The Gift of Struggle

by Bobby Herrera

Bard Press

Austin · Portland

About the Author

Bobby Herrera is cofounder and CEO of Populus Group. With annual revenue of $500 million and many Fortune 100 customers, it is one of the fastest-growing HR services companies in the United States.

Bobby grew up on the outskirts of a small town in New Mexico. As one of thirteen children in a migrant family he learned the value of hard work, rising early and putting in long hours in the fields. After high school, boot camp became his ticket of opportunity.

He serves on national community organization boards and is a regular speaker at corporations and service groups. He is a proud Army veteran.

Bobby is most proud of his family. His wife Roslyn and their three children Santino, Griffith, and Sofia live in Portland, Oregon.

Table of Contents

1. The Bus Story 1
2. Struggle and Gifts 5

Part One: Who Am I?

3. Your Leadership Journey — Tell Your Story 17
4. The Phone Call — Choose the Hardest Right 29
5. Road Trip — Share What You Imagine 41

Part Two: Give > Take

6. The Demotion — Own Your Part 55
7. Dr. Joe — Always Be a Student 67
8. The T-Chart — Ask Better Questions 79
9. The Meeting — Speak from the Heart 91

Part Three: Choose Your Impact

10. Hiking with the Kids — Go off the Beaten Path 103
11. Desert Shower — More Is Not the Answer 115
12. Rainier — Not Everyone Will Summit 129
13. The Toy Pile — Work as One 141

14. Become a Student of Struggle 153

Pay It Forward: A Guide for Leaders
Using *The Gift of Struggle* 161

Guides to Help You Learn from Struggle 166
Acknowledgments 168
Copyright 171

Chapter 1

The Bus Story

When I was 17, my brother Ed and I played on the same high school basketball team. Returning from an away game one night on the team bus, we all talked excitedly, reliving the highlights of the game we had just won. Along the way, the bus stopped at a restaurant so the team could unload and eat dinner. Everyone filed out—except for Ed and me.

My brother and I couldn't afford to buy meals on school trips. Instead, our mom would send us off with her legendary burritos so we could still participate in sports with the other kids. Eating on the bus was routine. We were long past any embarrassment we might have felt.

Minutes after the team had gone, we were about to dig into our dinner. Unexpectedly, Mr. Teague, the father of a teammate, reboarded the bus. He didn't say much at first—just teased me a bit because my younger brother had outscored me in the game. But I'll always remember what he said next.

"Bobby," he said, "it would make me very happy if you would allow me to buy you boys dinner so you can join the rest of the team. No one else has to know. To thank me, you just have to do the same thing in the future for another great kid like yourself."

That small gesture had a profound impact on me. As a family of migrant workers, I had felt from a very young age that we were socially invisible. I lived in a country that relied on my family's work for readily available food, but no one acknowledged what we did. Our family traveled six months of the year to work in the fields, and I inevitably returned home to find that my friends' lives had moved on, leaving me anxious to reconnect and catch up on the fun-filled summer I had missed.

As a high school junior, I couldn't imagine that I would live a life different from the one I had, but I was dead set on not getting stuck where I was. As a resilient kid with the desire to take control of my own story, I realized I had to get my life together—and fast. When my dad would tease that he would "break my plate" when I graduated, it wasn't really a joke. I would soon be on my own.

That day on the bus I was seen in a new and important way. I knew my parents loved me. I had teachers and coaches who had taken the time to encourage and cultivate me. But Mr. Teague was different. He was a successful businessman in our town. In my eyes, he was someone who had made it big—definitely not the type of person I expected to pay attention to me. And yet he not only acknowledged me but also offered kindness and gave me a purpose. In a simple statement, Mr. Teague said that I could one day help somebody else who really needed it, like I had.

I'll never forget the gratitude I felt as Ed and I joined the team for dinner that night. It changed the way I looked at my life and what I wanted to achieve.

STRUGGLE:
(v)
TO STRIVE TO ACHIEVE OR ATTAIN SOMETHING IN THE FACE OF DIFFICULTY OR RESISTANCE

Chapter 2

Struggle and Gifts

I have told the bus story to countless groups, and people always come up to me afterwards to tell me how much hearing that story mattered to them. Many tell me they have a bus story of their own. Maybe you do too.

As a kid from the wrong side of the opportunity divide, I can tell you that there was only one thing that mattered to me: I wanted to get off the bus. I wanted the same opportunities that I saw all around me. That was my struggle.

Struggle is painful. Whatever our individual circumstances, we all understand struggle as part of the human condition. It can be demoralizing and defeating when you make a mistake or simply become stuck and don't know where to turn. It's publicly humiliating when you can't hide your failure from others. Nonetheless, my advice for anyone with the courage to do so is to make struggle your best friend. Although it's uncomfortable, it's the most honest and revealing measure of progress toward becoming the leader you desire to be.

To understand my journey with struggle, I would like to tell you a story about my dad.

His Struggle

In the spring of 1954 my dad, Jorge, waited in line at a reception center in northern Mexico as he had been doing every spring for years. There were millions more like him across Mexico, waiting day after day to be selected as a *bracero*. Braceros were manual laborers, their name coming from the Spanish word meaning "one who works with his arms." The Bracero Program was an agreement between the United States and Mexico that began in 1942 and continued until 1964. It was created to supply temporary labor to the United States, offsetting worker shortages during World War II.

While millions waited, only 300,000 were chosen
to become contract workers that year. As a teenager,
my father had set his heart on joining the military,
but family hardships had made it impossible.
After missing that opportunity, he was determined
to become a bracero. He had to wait for nine years,
but my father was finally selected.

As a bracero, my dad performed long hours of
backbreaking work harvesting produce throughout
the western United States, leaving his wife and
young children behind in Mexico for months at a
time. Enduring harsh conditions, he earned less
than $1 an hour. Though he always tried to protect
me from knowing the worst of his experiences,
I know now that housing and sanitation were
typically substandard (if not squalid) and food was
inadequate—conditions that violated the braceros'
contract agreements. But that didn't seem to matter.
Treatment of laborers in the field was often brutal.

During the last days of his life, my dad told me
that the day he became a bracero was the day he
won *la lotería*—the lottery. Knowing what he had
been through, I was more than a little confused

by his words. I would have expected anger at the deprivation, ill treatment, and low wages he was forced to endure. But my dad had a different perspective. His mother, my abuelita, was rescued off the streets after being orphaned as a baby girl. Growing up in Chihuahua, mired in intergenerational poverty, my dad's single-minded aim was to end his family's cycle of impoverishment. He would offer his own children something more than he had. There was no sacrifice too great and no condition too harsh for him to bear when it came to providing for us.

Our Struggle

In 1964, my mother, Martina, and my brothers and sisters immigrated to the United States with my dad when the Bracero Program ended. I joined the family four years later and was the first sibling to be born in the United States. My parents settled in southeast New Mexico, where my dad worked on a sheep ranch. We lived in a small two-bedroom home filled with love but very few luxuries. Of the thirteen kids in our family, I was one of the youngest.

From an early age I grew accustomed to waking at 5:00 a.m. to work, whether in the fields with my siblings as a migrant farm family or with my dad in our small ranch community. Working before and often after school was our way of life.

Every spring my family left school in April and headed to Colorado, Wyoming, and Idaho. We harvested onions, potatoes, and pears and weeded sugar beet fields. By September, we were back in school, wearing the new school clothes we bought with money we earned, trying to catch up on the lessons we had missed. As a young child, I began working to contribute to the family. I would still get time to play and roam with my younger brother Ed, but work eventually evolved to six days a week and ten hours a day in the cotton fields of New Mexico and Texas as I grew older. What was normal for me seemed as if it was normal for everyone.

By the time I reached junior high, though, I was aware that while my hardworking parents were doing their best, the difference between our family and others around us was plain to see. Though I never felt ashamed, I was very defensive of what others might know or say about us. When my mom sent me to buy milk, I hid behind the grocery store dumpster and only went in to buy what we needed right before closing so no one would see me pay with food stamps. When I stood in line for school lunches, I devised a comical routine of distracting the kids around me so they wouldn't notice the attendant checking my name off the free lunch list. It was a game of saving face, which I played in order to make our family look the same as everyone else's.

Struggle as a Gift

It wasn't until I was eighteen, in the Army and three weeks into boot camp, polishing my boots by flashlight at 11:30 p.m., that I began to re-evaluate my upbringing. Surrounded by members of my new platoon, I found that most of the others were unprepared for long hours of drills, the sergeant's demeaning profanity, and the systematic breakdown of everything we thought to be true about ourselves. As everyone around me that night complained about waking up at 4:30 a.m. to start the next torturous day of training, I realized it was not that different from the life I had lived at home. I had already endured years of labor in the fields, rising before dawn. I had already encountered blatant racism, and I was already accustomed to living without material comforts or much free time.

That night it occurred to me that what I had already experienced was as tough as what I would face in the next few months. For the first time, having struggled early in life was turning out to be an advantage. It felt like a gift not to worry whether I would make it through basic training. I never questioned whether I could handle the grueling physicality and mental strain demanded from new recruits. I simply needed to draw on the persistence, strength, and resilience I already had.

I was grateful for the sacrifices my parents had made, but it took longer to internalize that my dad—a humble, powerful peasant—had accomplished his goal for our family. Even though it didn't feel like it as a kid, he had succeeded in providing opportunities for his children that were never available to him.

Eventually I began to study in earnest what struggle had taught me, why I should be grateful for it, and how I could apply the lessons it offered. In each case, struggle gave me a gift. I realized that I could often look back to an event from my past to find the clarity I needed. When I found myself facing a new challenge, my life experience could provide a new story and a crucial lesson to add to what I knew.

You Never Know . . .

Years later I called Mr. Teague to share the life-altering impact of that moment of altruism on the bus. I shared the inspiration I drew from that experience to pay forward his kind act. He was deeply touched. A few days later a note arrived from him thanking me for the call and admitting it had brought tears to his eyes. He told me that my call made him feel that his life had mattered.

Many people have told me that they see themselves as that kid on the bus; they remember how it felt to be invisible. Even more people tell me about becoming the generous, observant person who notices a kid being left out. You might offer something as simple as listening to their story and taking the time to recognize them for who they are. We never know how a single kind act might alter the day—or the life—of a struggling kid who crosses our path.

Part One

Who Am I?

Your Leadership Journey
Tell Your Story

The Phone Call
Choose the Hardest Right

Road Trip
Share What You Imagine

Chapter 3

Your Leadership Journey

In this book, I share my stories of struggle and self-doubt, but this book is really about *your* journey. Although your path will be different, in the end we all want the same thing: to believe our life matters. We all want our potential to be recognized, and we all want to be given the opportunity to excel.

I also believe that most of us have a pivotal story—an experience containing the gift of struggle that begs to be told. The story may be a turning point or an "Aha!" moment that gave us purpose. For most leaders, their ambition stems from something profoundly personal, something much deeper than the prospect of financial gain.

But because it's so central to who they are, it's intimidating to broadcast and share that struggle.

The Magic of Story

I cofounded Populus Group (PG) in 2002, a service firm that helps companies better manage their non-permanent workforce. Populus is the Latin word for "people," and at our core we believe everyone deserves an opportunity to succeed. The trouble was I had never helped the people at PG understand *why* I had such an intense passion to succeed.

Several years ago I was in the middle of a huge project, creating a presentation to explain and codify our culture—why we exist, how we behave, and what we are committed to as a company. As I was filming the video portion of the presentation, I recited one of our core principles: "We believe everyone deserves an opportunity to succeed."

The videographer, a quiet guy named Ben, looked up from his camera and asked, "Why do you believe that?" For reasons I still don't completely comprehend, I answered the question. I told him the bus story as the camera kept recording. Telling the story, unrehearsed and unplanned, was an enormous relief to me.

The next year, the entire company heard the bus story for the first time as part of the presentation. The story resonated in a remarkable way, and people began telling their own marker stories to one another. In time, sharing those stories deepened workplace bonds as empathy and compassion grew, making it easier for people to connect and work together.

Once everyone understood my purpose for creating PG, it gave their work purpose too. Everyone saw the value and promise of a company committed to underwriting opportunities for kids who started out like me. The detachment I had felt from my employees started to diminish as we all aligned around a common goal. To the people of PG, my intensity finally made sense; sharing my story had humanized me. They knew who I really was, what I cared about, and what I wanted to be known for.

I've been asked many times why I didn't share my story sooner. Part of my reluctance had stemmed from the idea that no one needed to hear it or that no one would want to know. My real struggle was opening up, being vulnerable, and letting everyone see the real me. Sharing the bus story revealed my own deepest doubts: Am I worthy? Will I ever be more than that struggling boy on the bus? To me, the stakes seemed perilously high. If I worked up the nerve to tell my most foundational story and was rejected, where would that leave me? However, it's a leader's responsibility to tell that story and to allow the narrative and its significance to work its magic and give greater meaning to the work people do.

Leadership Is an Inside Job

As a leader, this is your responsibility. Your job is to recognize that the people you lead want to participate in meaningful work. They want to feel that their role is respected and contributes to the advancement of a greater good. To supply that, you must see them the way Mr. Teague saw me. When an employee knows they matter, you inspire them to become better at what they do and more confident in who they are.

It was immensely difficult to start a business and gain footing as a leader. Believing worn-out clichés only made things harder. I put ridiculous pressure on myself to have all the answers. I thought I needed to cultivate the façade of executive detachment, that I had to be the guy at the top of the organizational chart that always had his act together. Previous work experiences and cultural stereotypes provided no shortage of bad or unrealistic examples to follow. I emulated the ego-driven, self-important alpha boss for far too long. I would have been better served in those years had I simply been guided by my dad's example of humility and sacrifice.

With time I found generous mentors who helped me identify my knowledge gaps. They asked tough questions and called on me to account for my thickheaded assumptions. I still rely on the indispensable wisdom of my trusted advisors. But as leaders, our dreams, our organizations, and our choices are unique. Every successful leader will be required to leave the familiar behind and strike out on their own in order to realize their vision. Inevitably, we all feel the heavy weight we carry on our shoulders and realize how lonely it can be.

Leadership is not a function of gender, color, wealth, or education. As my own story makes clear, I didn't come from a privileged background. No matter their starting point in life, every leader soon discovers what we all share—struggle is the most honest and revealing measure of progress toward becoming the leader you desire to be.

Patrick Lencioni, bestselling author and founder of The Table Group, says the true work of leadership is always an inside job; it's all about building character. For this reason, the most important question we can ask ourselves is, "Who am I becoming?"

We all struggle.
Inside every struggle is a gift.
Leaders share their gifts with others.

The Gift:
Tell Your Story

If you don't step up and tell the story that gives
you identity and purpose, your people will be
left on their own, trying to guess what matters
to you and why. Without fulfilling work, they
will make assumptions about your mission—or lack
thereof—and leave when they find a competitor
who offers what you've withheld. Until then,
they'll give you just enough to check the box and
get through the day.

For those of you who choose to take the leap,
you have to be all in. Your story must be clear,
and your message must be honed. People will
know the difference between the truth and a bluff.
Only transparency will pay the dividend of
stronger connections and shared goals within
an organization.

It won't happen overnight, but the whole idea
is to overcommunicate your story. Take every
opportunity to share with your team how they
are helping to achieve your biggest dream.
This will give them a new level of engagement

and pride in being part of something greater than themselves. In return, acknowledge and honor the stories that your people share with you and with one another. Celebrate the milestones they achieve. Just like you and me, they want to be seen and know they are worthy.

Questions to Guide
Your Journey

1. Do the people you lead know the story that drives you?

2. How is this story embedded in everything you do?

3. How are you encouraging your people to share their most important story?

Flash-Forward

The project I was working on when I first shared the bus story became the first version of PG's "Culture Code." Our Culture Code shares principles and values that everyone in PG agrees to live by in order to bring the story we want to create to life. My role is to narrate the story. I must guide the journey and tell that story over and over again. Eight years have passed since that initial project, and we are now on Version 3.0 of our Culture Code. Following it can be a challenging endeavor; like any good story, there is the unpredictable element of human behavior. In Chapter 5, I share more about my inspiration for our Culture Code.

\- \- \-

Chapter 4

The Phone Call

My sister was on the other end of the line. "You may want to come home and see Dad," she said. She had reached me on a business trip to Vancouver, British Columbia, in the spring of 1998. Our father had been rushed to the hospital. He'd been fighting tuberculosis for eighteen months, and we all recognized there wasn't much time left.

I referred to my dad as "the Mexican John Wayne," and we had watched him confront this disease in his typical stoic manner. He wore a cowboy hat and boots all his life and lived by the code of his generation: men don't cry, and they don't show fear. As a boy, I rarely left his side. He was a conquistador in my eyes, but that didn't mean it was always easy to be close to my dad. He was a study in contradictions: charismatic, affectionate, stubborn, and impatient. As Mom would say, he was either honey or poison.

I was scheduled to fly to Colorado Springs that weekend to attend a friend's wedding. I had also booked a flight to New Mexico to visit my parents on Sunday after the wedding. It would be easy enough to rearrange my plans, skip the wedding, and get to the hospital the next day.

Early the next morning, I called my dad. I wanted to hear his voice and reassure him I was on the way and would be arriving that evening. But there was only silence on the other end of the line— my dad's patented . . . long . . . pause. I was baffled. Silence from Dad signaled disagreement with a choice I was making. What could possibly be wrong with coming to see him, especially now?

When he finally spoke, he asked in Spanish, "Don't you have a wedding to go to in Colorado this weekend?"

"*Sí*, Papa. But my friend will understand. He knows how sick you are."

Another long pause.

"Did you give him your word?"

"*Sí*, Papa, but he'll understand."

Silence. Again.

To fill the intolerable void, I started arguing like a teenager who wants to borrow the car. But there was no amount of pleading that would change my father's mind. To drive home the point, he proceeded to tell me (in colorful Spanish) that I was welcome to change my plans, but if I showed up, he wouldn't allow me in his hospital room.

Knowing his mind was made up, I reluctantly kept my plans to attend the wedding. I was pissed, confused, frustrated, and scared to death that I wouldn't get there to see him in time.

Few things mattered to my dad more than honoring your word. If you gave it, you kept it, no matter what. He fiercely protected this principle because for most of his life, his word was the only thing of value he had. He'd made sure that all of us kids knew that he expected the same from us.

As I flew to the wedding in Colorado Springs, I second-guessed my decision, certain I would always regret my choice. Telling myself I should have defied my dad, I kept thinking, *"There's no way he wouldn't let me in the room."* I braced myself for the regret of never seeing him again.

When I arrived at the hotel in Colorado Springs, I settled in and called Dad. He told me to have a good time. "Come home Sunday," he said. "I'll be here waiting for you."

Three days later, I finally exhaled when I walked into his hospital room. I'd kept my word, and my dad had kept his.

- - -

The Gift:
Choose the Hardest Right

In PG's eleventh year, the robust growth of the previous five years slowed to a near standstill. I was nervous, flipping every stone, wondering if the good times had been a fluke. The forensics I performed frustrated me even more. I wasn't uncovering anything abnormal in the business. We had gaps in some areas, but there were no major issues. We picked up a little momentum in the next few months, but I still couldn't identify why

I was so uneasy.

I believed the conventional wisdom that the future of the company depended on our industry expertise and quality of work. You must create value. I placed great emphasis on leading my team to drive results. I was accountable for the big stuff, but I would occasionally let little things slide because I thought keeping my eye on the prize— the bottom line—was far more important.

On top of that, I didn't have the type of connection I wanted to have with my team. I craved relationships in which we trusted each other implicitly, like my dad and I trusted each other, enough to follow each other anywhere. Instead, PG's office associations were all on the surface.

Unable to piece together what was right in front of me, I hired an outside consultant to facilitate an off-site meeting. The consultant revealed all the ways we weren't showing up for each other. We didn't call each other back, we were constantly late, and we chased after each other for needed information. The tension in the room during the meeting was thick.

As I listened, I kept returning to the story about

my dad holding me to my word and insisting that I attend my friend's wedding. Intuitively, I finally understood how all the problems connected: the slowdown in the business; the lack of cohesion across the company; the flaw of only caring about expertise, work product, and profit. All of this struggle hinged on my failure to keep my word.

The success of the previous five years had distracted me from doing what successful leadership requires. The little things in your day start to seem like no big deal. "I'm only a few minutes late to the meeting, but they know I'm busy." "I didn't call that client back, but I'll do it later." "The report will be late, but next week is good enough." You have good intentions, so you assume your lapses are harmless, and besides—you're the boss.

As a leader, everyone watches and listens to you, ready to make judgments. When there's a gap between what you say and what you do, it undermines your integrity, making it harder for people to trust you. Both employees and clients keep a tally of your actions. Your behaviors, more than your words, will set the tone and example that everyone else will follow.

If you have failed to build trust as a leader, you can still earn the confidence of your people and clients. Have conversations with your leaders and the entire company. Tell them you will no longer allow little things to slide. Don't blame or dodge; take full responsibility for your company's circumstances. Promise to call out mistakes respectfully, and ask others to do the same for you.

Incorporate a trust-building signal into your interactions. For example, the appointments I set for calls with my team members start at unusual times like 8:29 or 11:02, never the top or bottom of the hour. The psychological benefit of this practice is that by calling at precisely that minute, it sends the signal that I keep my word.

Emphasize the importance of daily behaviors that build trust—practicing candor, listening first, keeping promises, and creating transparency, to name a few. We learn many of these things as kids. Affirm what we all know and practice those behaviors at the office. Hammer home that trust must be established before anyone will listen to your message, believe in your value proposition, choose your services, or stick with you when times get tough.

Don't put the value of a dollar before the necessity of trust. Don't undermine your integrity and assume the little things are invisible. Everyone can see what your character is like. You can hide from yourself, but you'll never fool your team. The trust people have in you is the most important asset you will ever own. It's either a headwind or a tailwind that will make or break your company, your brand, your reputation, and your ability to lead.

We're far from perfect at PG. I pointedly call out our errors when we miss opportunities to win one another's trust or our clients'. We celebrate moments when we achieve the trust-building goals we set, even when sticking to our commitments is excruciatingly hard. With diligence, we've transformed our company into a community, replacing superficial relationships with a supportive and collaborative environment. The dramatic change across the company is a gift, the result of making trust the most important thing we measure.

Questions to Guide
Your Journey

1. How are you modeling fundamental behaviors that build trust?

2. How are you intentionally building trust with your team?

3. What metric do you care about the most?

Flash-Forward

When I arrived at the hospital following the wedding in Colorado Springs, I spent the week at my dad's bedside, holding his broad, strong hand and listening to his stories when he had the energy to talk. I asked a lot of questions, knowing our conversations would soon end. But I also had a new story to tell.

The night before the wedding I was having a beer with a friend, catching up on the latest news. A friend of his came over to say hello—a beautiful, gray-eyed Norwegian girl. My friend introduced us, but after I heard, "Bobby, this is Roslyn," I don't remember anything else that was said. She stuck around for a while as I attempted to conceal the fact that I was just a nervous kid inside. I don't believe in fate, but later that evening I wondered if my dad knew I needed to be in Colorado Springs to meet this woman from Seattle.

I never talked with my dad about women I dated, but I knew this one was different, and I told him all about her. During our final days together, I had the chance to thank him in person for showing me the importance of honoring my word. He had risked not seeing me one last time in order to reinforce an unforgettable lesson. He passed away three weeks later on May 20, 1998.

Three years later, I married Roslyn. I like to tell people that my dad saved his best gift for last.

Kalamazoo 23

Detroit 165

Chapter 5

Road Trip

Roslyn and I made a cross-country trip from San Jose, California, to Detroit, Michigan, in 2002. Recently married, we were literally driving toward a brand new life. We left everything familiar behind us and looked forward to a new home, new city, and new friends. But what loomed large on the road ahead wasn't the scenery but rather the prospect of starting my own company.

Roslyn and I were going for broke with this new venture. Our emotions rode the roller coaster from excitement to dread and everything in between. Though she was completely supportive, my wife asked a lot of questions, like what the plan was for success. Her thinking exemplified one big difference between us. I'm an organizational nightmare and a part-time cowboy. I'm comfortable with the Wild West mentality—taking the reins in a world with few settled boundaries, meeting challenges as they arise. But Roslyn is a planner. She wants to know what's coming and how to prepare for it.

As her questions continued, I became less and less capable of answering with any confidence. Unnerved, I was unable to supply clear, concrete responses given the difficulty of anticipating the reality of the new company.

After a period of silence, about a hundred miles outside of Detroit, Roslyn asked the easiest question I've ever answered.

"Are you scared?"

"I'm terrified."

In reality, I wanted a business that was the opposite of much of the businesses I'd been a part of as an employee. We both had experienced episodes at work when we didn't feel heard, valued, or worse . . . relevant. My laundry list of top offenses included things most people hate as much as I do: office drama, backstabbing, gossip, lying, and corporate politics. I especially didn't like bosses who pretended to know more than they did. Everyone could always see right through them.

I shifted the conversation from everything I didn't want to think about to explaining how the company would "feel" someday. I wanted people to connect to a purpose larger than themselves. I wanted to create an environment where everyone knew their worth and could be themselves instead of "just pretending." Like a scrappy team, we would fight like hell to win, knowing we had each other's backs, no matter what. I wanted us to always tell the truth, even when it was difficult or scary to do so. Like curious, unassuming kids, I didn't want us to take ourselves too seriously. I wanted our work to include creative fun, play, and mischief. I wanted us to be humble and remain students of our craft, no matter what our titles were. Lastly, I told Roslyn, we'd be a company devoted to continually learning from the wisdom of exceptional leaders.

By the end of my wild rant, we had nearly reached Detroit.

"How in the world are you going to do all that?" Roslyn asked.

I laughed. "I have no freaking idea. Trust me, though . . . I'll find a way."

- - -

The Gift:
Share What You Imagine

Somehow, I thought the people I led would know what I was trying to build. I thought they would discern the whole picture from what I attempted to show them every day and automatically extrapolate from there. But if my first error was trying to create the company culture I imagined without explaining it to anyone, the follow-up assumption made it drastically worse. I shouldered the burden of establishing culture as though it was my responsibility alone, and by doing so, I magnified my struggle.

The first five years at PG were turbulent and exciting, but sometimes things really sucked. Once we officially opened our doors, culture—while not entirely forgotten—became secondary to staying alive. The distractions only grew as the inevitable conflicts of starting a business increased. We fought to survive and execute the grand business plan we wrote prior to launching the company. The lead-up to the 2008 recession intensified all the challenges a young, unproven company confronts.

The economic pressure created serious tension between the founding partners and me. We dissolved our partnership between 2005 and 2008, a financially painful but amicable event. Ending the partnership generated the kind of distraction, tension, and drama I despise. PG strayed ever further from that original, sublime plan.

The silver lining was that I now was the sole owner of the company's culture. I was exhausted from the start-up years, but the turbulence started to level off. At last I saw exciting potential. But the culture—the environment I described on the road to Detroit years before—still didn't exist.

I slowly came to the disheartening realization that my company had a culture; it just wasn't the one I intended. Reading everything I could find, I became aware that if I didn't supply the vision, we were never going to arrive at the place I imagined.

Introducing the culture I wanted was going to require a kind of focus and energy that I had no idea how to generate.

Culture means different things to different people, and the more imprecise the definition is, the harder it becomes to act on. For me, culture is simple: it's the feeling people get when they interact with your company. For example, how do you feel when you go to Disneyland? How does Nordstrom's service make you feel? The product is the result of a set of standards, practices, and attitudes. But culture is also experiential, the hook that keeps us coming back. "Brand" is a lagging indicator of the strength of the culture. I tend to agree.

Successful organizations and winning teams are intentional about what they cultivate. Nordstrom and Disneyland are passionate about customer service; Southwest Airlines shows an unrelenting commitment to their business recipe; the New Zealand All Blacks and the US Navy SEALs are devoted to continuous improvement and producing great leaders. These organizations don't allow "ROE" ("return on ego") to compromise the integrity of the culture. Enduring cultures are never enforced by a top-down hierarchy. Everyone lives the culture, and therefore everyone must use their voice to contribute to it.

Rigor and determination are required to bring the culture you dream of to life. To execute the culture you envision, you must focus on the following key areas:

1. Build Identity: Become fanatical about making sure everyone knows the vision of the culture, its purpose, and what it means to be a community member.

2. Guide Behavior: Overcommunicate exactly how you expect everyone who is part of the culture to behave. Encourage your leaders to be unwavering in their demands about the company's principles.

3. Speak a Common Language: Use common vernacular—a language everyone can remember that is authentic to your organization—and craft your message to reinforce the first two points.

Building culture is more "how" than "what." To build a healthy culture, you must establish a few guiding principles that set expectations for behavior and performance within the company and with clients. At PG, we honor the following three principles that everyone must follow:

- Give more than you take.
- Speak from the heart.
- Go off the beaten path.

They are not *rules*—and that's the trick. They are *guidelines* that reinforce our belief that collaboration, honesty, and innovation ground and sustain culture. By stating boundaries in the positive case, they are expansive, not restrictive. As a leader, the guiding principles you choose should also allow you to identify and reward behaviors that bring your core values to life.

Every leader wants a strong, resilient culture that frees the organization to do its best work. The strength of the culture governs the strength of the connection between the people you lead. Leaders must supply an unshakable vision for the culture they wish to build, whether they lead a small team or an entire organization. But determining the culture—setting the course—doesn't mean you can build and sustain it all on your own. The guidelines you select have to be understood and embraced by everyone within the organization, creating a virtuous cycle.

I believe most leaders have a big imagination and a bright vision for how their company culture should guide and engage their employees. If you're a leader, describe your daring dream to those around you. Don't attempt to build it by yourself. Tell the story, describe the feeling, and define and protect the boundaries. Your people are human. Just like you, they will forget. Kindly remind them of your vision every chance you get. Do this consistently, and over time your talented, receptive people will bring to life a vision more brilliant than anything you could've imagined.

- - -

Questions to Guide
Your Journey

1. What is your vision for the company culture and why?

2. How does your culture make people feel?

3. What great organizations or teams can you learn from to strengthen your culture?

Flash-Forward

Another big question for us on that road trip
was how this decision would impact the future we
had imagined together. Two months prior, Rosyln
and I were having our final conversation about
starting PG. We had a decision to make. She sat
quietly as I shared with her one final detail.
"If we do this, we will have to leave California
and move to Detroit."

She just stared for a moment before finally saying,
"Honey, it's cold in Detroit!"

Like any good husband does, I immediately tried
to recover. I said, "Give me five years in Detroit,
and I promise to get you back to the West Coast."
(I had no idea how in the world I would do that—
I was reaching.) But she agreed.

We moved back five and a half years later . . .
and she's given me credit for keeping my promise.

- - -

Part Two

Give > Take

The Demotion
Own Your Part

Dr. Joe
Always Be a Student

The T-Chart
Ask Better Questions

The Meeting
Speak from the Heart

Chapter 6

The Demotion

"Bobby, I don't think you're a good business person. Since you don't seem to know what a good director looks like, we're going to put you back into a sales role."

Those words stung and infuriated me beyond belief. I'd been promoted to a regional management role overseeing the West Coast region of a big company. I had five hundred people reporting to me from fifteen offices. I'd built a strong reputation in prior years running offices in two key markets.

I was certain I could handle the new promotion, but less than a year into my new role, the financials plunged across the board. I was called to corporate headquarters for a reckoning with the boss. I was in good company, at least. Six other regional managers hadn't hit their targets either. They were reassigned as well.

I replayed my boss's comments in my head, countering them. *"I don't know what a good director looks like? What the hell did that mean? I had been considered one of the best before my promotion!"*

I kept going. *"Not a good business person? Don't you know about my finance and accounting background? Of course not . . . you don't know anything about my story. You only called me twice in the year I reported to you. You didn't teach me a freaking thing about the job!"* I was finding every reason to blame.

As disappointed as I felt, I was too angry to quit. I didn't know why I was so upset, but I knew I didn't want my story there to end that way.

My new lesser role still had a steep learning curve. I was a pretty good salesperson, but I knew I needed to hone my craft. My new boss was similar to my old boss, so I wasn't expecting much help there. Determined not to repeat history, I had to be honest with myself.

I reluctantly admitted I hadn't been insistent about asking for help. Instead, I relied on calls to my struggling peers that were more about venting than learning. Though a more experienced peer had taken time to show me the ropes when he could, I'd been too proud to admit I needed more guidance.

A few months into my new sales role, I became aware of a VP of sales at an up and coming start-up who had an amazing reputation. After learning more about her, I called to ask if she would become my mentor. It took five calls and numerous letters, but she finally agreed to meet for breakfast. I made the right impression and earned another session with her.

She quickly figured out that I had virtually zero experience in this type of sales role. By the end of that first meeting, I recall thinking, *"Maybe I'm not as good a business person as I thought?"* She recommended that I attend a week-long sales executive course at the University of Chicago.

I made the request to my new boss. It was quickly denied, but I was still determined to find a way to attend the course. Using my vacation hours and my own money, I flew to Chicago for the week. When I returned, I met with my new mentor, and she helped me put what I learned at school into action. The harder I worked at applying what she taught me, the more I found her willing to help me. My confidence rebounded, and the results showed in my work.

The Gift:
Own Your Part

In 2011, PG was hit with a wave of attrition that lasted for eighteen very long months. I was anxious to be losing people like we were. I started hating going to the office on Fridays because it meant someone was going to quit. I vividly recall having a conversation with a person in the company, a friend of another employee who had unexpectedly resigned. She offered the great kindness of being candid with me. "Bobby," she said, "I'm very thankful for everything you and PG have done for me, but you don't see what we see. We know you care, even though you're intense, but at PG it often feels like it's all about getting stuff done and hitting our numbers."

She was right. It was hurtful and hard to hear, but I knew that somehow I was at fault. I was at a decision point again, just like when I was demoted, only this time, I couldn't quit the company I cofounded—even if I wanted to. But more important, the demotion struggle had given me a gift: it showed me we all play a role in any problem or conflict we deal with. We may not be solely responsible for it, and we can't control everything, but rest assured that in some way or form, we contribute all the same.

As leaders, we set the tone for how everyone in the organization is guided. I was modeling a style of leadership that failed me earlier in my career. Patience didn't come easily for me. I wanted to think I was different from other aspiring leaders, but as I reflected on what she shared, I realized that in the early years I was inconsistent, moody, and lacking in empathy. I genuinely wanted to help people improve and achieve great things, but when I handed off a new responsibility to someone, I expected them to dive in, suck it up, and be fearless.

I was experiencing the dilemma an early mentor had taught me: intent versus impact. What my employee shared with me wasn't what I intended, but the impact I was making—and what I was teaching my leaders by default—was too much like that of my former boss. My leaders were left to sink or swim, as I had been, and the fall-out was cascading throughout the rest of the organization.

I braced myself for the course correction I was about to make and went to work. First, I made a list of the last ten people I'd promoted and asked myself the following simple questions:

- How did I set up a new leader to succeed?
- How did I start their leadership journey?
- How did I transition the teams?

That exercise told me everything I needed to know, presenting a clear picture of how we guided people. My leaders were frantically trying to get things done, but I was tossing them overboard without a life preserver. I may as well have said, "Here you go! A new title and more responsibility— good luck!" As a result, we were making too many tactical mistakes, teams weren't communicating, and my new leaders weren't developing their people.

The mistakes were frustrating our customers and impacting the trust we had worked so hard to earn.

I had no choice but to be patient, a monumental task for me in and of itself. I had a lot of well-intentioned people who were new to their leadership roles. It wasn't fair or realistic to think that I could change things overnight. I needed to slow things down and teach them exactly how I wanted them to behave, which meant doing more than just telling them. It meant showing them too.

I invested more time with my leaders and really got to know them. I made sure everyone understood the impact I wanted us to have on our teams. I worked hard to model, albeit imperfectly, how helping someone with good-faith generosity was a better way to meet our goals than the hardcore approach I had demanded. What I set out to prove was that two seemingly contradictory goals were possible—that a caring and compassionate management strategy would be rewarding for us all and that we would still grow the business.

Over time, I eliminated or streamlined the training and tactical competencies that came with leadership promotions. While I believe competency matters, it doesn't matter as much as compassion and generosity. I made sure my leaders understood that compassion and generosity come first, and competency follows closely behind. As a leader, you must model this attitude for other leaders in your organization. You must be very curious about what people want in life, and help them build a plan to get there. It requires learning the best way to communicate with every person so you can find ways to stretch their potential without overwhelming them. Challenge people to do more than they believe they are capable of. Tell them the unvarnished truth while also telling them how much you believe in them.

Finally, and I can't over emphasize how important this is, encouragement and celebration every step of the way is critical, even when your people stray off course. Make them feel like you are always investing in their well-being. In my experience, the best way to do that is to catch them doing things right and recognize them over and over—recognition builds courage and confidence. As Patrick Lencioni often says, "People need to be

reminded more than they need to be instructed."
Leaders often lose their way by focusing more on
the bad than the good.

Ultimately, I switched my mindset. Just like
when I was demoted, I had to take responsibility
and own my part of the problem. Doing so helped
me learn that leadership amounts to wanting
more *for* our people than we want *from* them.
At PG, that means generosity and compassion
is the way we work. It's the best way we know
to cultivate great leaders and maintain a healthy
bottom line.

Questions to Guide
Your Journey

1. How are you showing your people that you want more for them than from them?

2. Do the leaders you guide know the mindset you expect them to have?

3. How are you embedding these expectations into your organization?

Flash-Forward

A few months after the course in Chicago, I was
doing well and focused on making my way back
up. There was a big shake-up at corporate and
my old boss was out. His replacement was a peer
who had helped me when I was in over my
head. He knew how determined I was to improve
and one day he said to me, "I'm shocked you
got the former president to approve that sales
course in Chicago." "He didn't," I replied. "I went
on my own dime." He paused a moment, quietly
thinking. Then we had a conversation about
what I had learned. We both knew that neither
one of us would have approved the course had
the situation been reversed. At the time of my
request, I hadn't earned the right to ask. At the
end of our conversation, he surprised me and
said he would make sure I was reimbursed for
the course.

- - -

Chapter 7

Dr. Joe

Dr. Joe is a gritty Sicilian, an industrial psychologist, and someone who doesn't have time for excuses. I met him in my late twenties when I was quickly rising through the ranks of a growing company. Due to the surge in company growth and rapid promotions, I had more responsibility and more people reporting to me than I was ready for.

Dr. Joe had been contracted to improve the leadership structure of the company. It was my first experience with an in-depth behavioral assessment, and I was skeptical. I didn't believe a test could come close to capturing who I was or how I operated.

When Dr. Joe reviewed the exam results with me a few weeks later, he was succinct and eerily precise. "You tend to do *this*. When you're frustrated you do *that*. The results show that you respond *this* certain way in *this* particular kind of situation." Everything he said was true, though not in a good way. Hearing it was about as pleasant as drinking vinegar.

"Bobby," he concluded, "you get distracted easily, and your discipline is very inconsistent. If you don't change, you're looking at your career ceiling— or you're pretty darn close to it already."

I felt completely naked. But at the same time, he offered what I needed. No one, other than my dad, made me feel the way Dr. Joe did. I wanted to trust him, but more than anything, I didn't want to disappoint him.

He laid out an assignment for me. "Read this book and call me so we can discuss everything you learned." That was the double dog dare I needed to prove to Dr. Joe that I could step up to the plate. I read the book and summarized the key takeaways. Brimming with confidence I called for our next appointment, certain I could win him over.

"Bobby, can you give me examples of exactly how you've applied what you learned?"

I didn't respond. Embarrassed, I racked my brain, but I couldn't think of anything I had actually changed.

"Bobby, please tell me how you've changed your behavior as a leader."

Again, I had nothing.

"If you want to be a wise leader someday, you must fiercely apply what you learn. You must also be selective when choosing who you will study." I probably heard the word "application" twenty more times that afternoon. I left more determined than ever to show the old Sicilian I could take anything he dished out.

He instructed me to read the book again and highlight only the parts that aligned with my leadership strengths. Next to the highlighted sections, he asked me to write down *exactly* how I was going to change my behavior and apply the lesson. Last of all, he said to me, "Brush your teeth with your weaker hand for thirty days. You need to learn what discomfort really feels like. The practice will teach you to think differently."

Reluctantly, I did. It wasn't a pretty sight.

The next time we met, I had been clumsily applying lessons taken from the book. The tasks included writing a heartfelt thank-you note once a week or asking people who thought differently than I did for their opinion. The exercises were simple, but they showed me how uncomfortable and difficult it was to change my behavior.

The Gift:
Always Be a Student

PG was three years old, and I was getting my ass kicked. For every account we'd win, we'd lose two others. Three of our first customers filed for bankruptcy early on. It was like walking on sand—impossible to build momentum. I was certain I was in over my head.

It had been nine years since I'd worked with Dr. Joe, but I'd just found another mentor who'd gotten me back on track. I met Bill at a networking event that I hadn't even wanted to attend. Although he was reluctant to meet with me at first, I got him to say yes. Bill looked exactly like what he is: a retired, gray-haired CEO. His first request was, "Don't make me feel like I'm wasting my time." I assured him I wouldn't and hoped I was right.

At our first breakfast meeting in Detroit, Bill asked confusing and pointed questions, like Dr. Joe had. "How do you behave in meetings?" "Tell me about your values." "Besides money, why did you start this company?"

My head was spinning. I had no idea how to answer any of these questions. As I stumbled over my responses, the only thing that captured his attention was the story about my vision for the culture I wanted to build. Bill finally shifted the conversation to what we did at PG. I was much more comfortable with this subject, but Bill was obviously bored as I rambled for half an hour. I knew he didn't care, but I kept talking to try and show him I was smart.

When I concluded my long-winded story, Bill's assessment sounded a lot like Dr. Joe's. Bill thought I had some potential, but he wasn't sure if I had the right mindset to run a healthy company. I was shocked. PG would be circling the drain if I didn't do something soon. For some reason the word "healthy" kept echoing in my mind.

Bill went on to add that I needed to simplify everything I'd told him, or I was going to be an average leader at best. "How am I going to do that?" I thought. He offered to meet again in a month if I read the book he recommended. I instantly agreed.

I picked up a copy of Patrick Lencioni's *The Four Obsessions of an Extraordinary Executive.* He makes the case that a leader's key role is to build a healthy organization that is unified rather than splintered by politics and infighting. The book describes how this often-overlooked element is a key to sustained success. Once I started reading the book, I couldn't put it down.

I followed the routine Dr. Joe had taught me. I read the book front to back and absorbed the information. Then I reread the book with Dr. Joe's voice in my head asking me, *"How will I change my behavior?"* Next, I highlighted the lessons that aligned with my strengths and wrote down how I would apply them.

This is where leaders lose their way. People think they can read a book and then somehow they've become better leaders. That couldn't be further from the truth. Until you apply what you have learned, you haven't started the journey toward improvement.

I persuaded Bill to meet me sooner than he wanted to. When we sat down together, I listed the changes I was going to make because of the reading I had done, and Bill offered guidance on what he'd learned applying the same lessons. For the first time, it felt like there was a connection between us. It brought home how I had neglected what I'd learned from Dr. Joe. I had lost sight of the practices that had given me the chance to build my own company in the first place.

When I started PG, I was distracted by the new and chaotic situation. There were more problems to solve than hours in the day. Being a real student felt like a luxury I couldn't afford when I was trying to keep the lights on in the early years.

My mistake was assuming that keen instincts and resilience were all I needed to be a successful leader. I reasoned that I could get ahead by being the first one in and the last one out of the office, believing I could outwork and out-charisma everyone. Although work ethic matters, and you must put in the time, it takes more than that to become a credible leader.

Academically I was solid, but like most of the world, I did just enough to get by. I knew the right buzz words to drop into conversations and could fake the rest. Even though I talked a good game, I knew it couldn't last. Meeting Bill was another wake-up call.

Your job as a leader isn't to have all the answers or be the expert. Rather, you must know your strengths and work rigorously and consistently to sharpen them. Most people understand that, but they don't commit to the task. Building on your strengths also highlights your weaknesses, allowing you to surround yourself with a team whose strengths complement, rather than duplicate, your own.

Bill taught me that a leader's strength and insight will only evolve if they remain consistent and identify new ways to learn and new people to learn from. Leaders must continually refresh their commitment by seeking other great teachers, like I did when I sought out Bill and he introduced me to Patrick Lencioni's work.

I'm grateful that my path crossed with Dr. Joe's. I'm also grateful Bill reinforced the necessity of being a real student. Above all, I'm grateful I finally realized my inconsistent approach would never work. I often see well-intentioned, high-potential leaders making the same mistake I have. They assume that what you read or study is what matters. It isn't. The real transformation is found in the application of what you learn.

I've been clumsily applying the knowledge I've gained from the best thought leaders in business since 2005. Over time I've incorporated what I most needed to know and developed my own leadership style. I credit these thought leaders for what they have given me, and I remain humble and on the hunt to identify new teachers.

Questions to Guide
Your Journey

1. How are you rigorously applying what you're studying to change your behavior?

2. How does what you're studying reinforce your strengths?

3. Who's the best thought leader that teaches what you need to learn?

Flash-Forward

The book Dr. Joe gave me sits on my "Bible Row" next to my desk, along with others that have shaped my behavior as a leader. It was my first John C. Maxwell read: *The 21 Irrefutable Laws of Leadership*. I've worked very hard to apply Maxwell's lessons over the years. Every month I pick a book from my Bible Row, review the notes that have guided me thus far, and assess how well I'm applying the book's lessons. I still randomly brush my teeth with my left hand as a reminder that being a student means getting comfortable with discomfort.

If you don't know which authors and experts to trust, ask a mentor or an experienced leader to help you identify who is worth reading. To get you started, a short list of my Bible Row can be found at the end of this book.

Chapter 8

The T-Chart

When my oldest son, Santino, was four, we noticed that his levels of frustration and aggravation were rising. My wife and I are fans of letting our kids struggle, but something wasn't right. He chewed his nails until they bled. His acting out was a growing concern.

By nature, Santino is crazy and fearless. He's the apple that didn't fall far from the tree. Whenever I got into trouble as a boy—which was too often— my dad would say to me, *"Hijo eres, Papa serás!"* In English, this means, "A son you are, a dad you'll be." Santino is single-handedly paying me back for all the mischief I stirred up as a kid. It was hard to watch the playful, spirited son we knew wrestle with his behavior and not know how to help him.

We asked our pediatrician for help, and he referred us to a child psychologist. After our initial meetings, we learned Santino was facing developmental challenges that affected his capacity to deal with frustration, which created very unhealthy levels of stress for him.

To help our son manage his condition, the psychologist sent us home with an exercise. He told us to take a sheet of paper and draw a large T across the top. The left-hand column would be labeled "Go" and the right column would be labeled "Stop." And then the psychologist asked my wife and me to track what kind of commands we gave our son. A Stop command was an instruction on what he couldn't do, like "Don't stand up in your chair at the table." A Go command was an instruction telling him what he could do, like "Please put your seat in the chair." Little did I know how this exercise would rock my soul to the core.

The next day we started tracking our commands. I found the majority of my instructions were Stop commands. The tick marks accumulated on the right side of the page. "Don't use your shirt to clean your hands." "Don't interrupt Mom and Dad while we're talking." On the second day, I literally broke down and cried. Our son was overwhelmed with frustration, and we just compounded his struggle by telling him over and over what he couldn't do.

We knew what had to change, though we quickly discovered how difficult it was to be more thoughtful when communicating with Santino. We worked hard to rephrase our Stop commands into Go commands. "Please use your napkin to wipe your hands." "Please wait patiently for us to stop talking and then ask your question." We only used a Stop command when it was safety related.

After three weeks, we noticed Santino's improvement. He was starting to act more like the boy we knew. He was less stressed, and in time he quit biting his nails. Even now we notice that when we regress and return to our old habits, Santino's behavior suffers too. It's an immediate reminder of the impact of our communication.

- - -

The Gift:
Ask Better Questions

Working on commands at home with Santino
inspired me to evaluate how things were going at
the office. I initiated individual conversations with
my team and asked how I made them feel during
tactical discussions. One leader told me I was
"quizzing" or "taking him down a rabbit hole" by the
way I asked questions. Another leader felt I didn't
trust their decision-making. Yet another confessed
to feeling like they were doing everything wrong
whenever we got off the phone. I was grateful they
trusted me enough to be honest with me.

I was disheartened and concerned. I had great
people that I trusted, and I loathed any hint of
micromanaging. If anything, I felt like I underman-
aged at times. But the exercise revealed that I held
people in check in a more subtle, imperceptible
way. I wanted to be encouraging while also
giving people the autonomy we all crave. I wanted
people to feel empowered when we spoke, not
deflated. If my questions and tone communicated
a lack of faith in people and their decisions, I

was simultaneously discouraging them and under-cutting the agency I wanted for them. I struggled with communicating in a dispiriting way, making the opposite of the positive impact and influence I wanted to convey.

When people ask a question, it contains two parts. There's the "what" part of the question: the words that come out of our mouths. There's also an unspoken "why": the reason for asking the question. The "what" is least important. Instead, it's better to focus on the "why." There's always a reason, whether it stems from a doubt, an insight, or a need for assistance that prompts a question. Most leaders don't respond to questions with discerning follow-up questions to better understand why the question was asked in the first place. As a leader, you need to get to the "why."

People generally won't say what really bothers them—they conceal the "why." In business, it's usually because someone sees the situation differently and has a concern, or they are missing information and don't want to reveal their knowledge gap. They are afraid of any circumstance that may reflect badly on them. If we don't acknowledge this dynamic in our conversations, we can't get past the confusion or frustration and move toward active solutions.

By instinct or training, often leaders know it's best to ask a lot of questions and do more listening. But the way you ask questions may be counter-productive, making people feel as though they have been caught doing something wrong. In turn, they aren't getting the helpful direction they need. As long as this condition continues, no one is going to feel encouraged or autonomous in their role. As a leader, I had to change the way my team felt every time I had a conversation with them.

I decided to tell the story of my experience with Santino. It was wrenching because it was such a hard lesson to learn as a dad. The twenty leaders I spoke to via conference call responded with prolonged silence. Rather than feeling awkward or uncomfortable, I got a sense of empathy and understanding. The team finally understood how deeply I wanted to encourage and energize each of them when we spoke.

To change the impression and impact you make in every conversation, from the water cooler to the boardroom, there are a few techniques to practice. When you need to clarify a question, paraphrase it and add a "why"—"This is what I hear you asking me *and why*." Be forthright and get to the most important part of any question early in the conversation. Another way to get to the root of "why" is to pay close attention to your tone and ask for elaboration using a phrase like, "Help me understand what you see a little better." The goal is to foster collaborative discussions that allow the whole organization to move forward.

Change your nonverbal language if you've developed bad habits. Even silence communicates volumes. If your body language is screaming, *"Are you freaking kidding me?"* you'll only undercut your intention to be supportive. Because 90% of communication is nonverbal, this is generally the hardest practice to change. But until you do, you'll be sending mixed messages, completely defeating your progress from the first two techniques.

An important benefit of this gift is how it leads to recognizing people for what they do well. As you become more encouraging in conversations, it's natural to reinforce positive behaviors you are trying to cultivate. Getting to "why" and using Go commands along with encouragement and recognition help satisfy a person's legitimate need to be appreciated and valued. The impact on happiness and engagement can't be matched. And it's free!

I believe the frustration we see in the eyes of those we are honored to lead is an invitation. Your role as a leader is to give people confidence every time you give direction. They must feel that you understand their reasoning, and you must question "why" until you do. Keep your powerful and unconscious body language in check, and don't leave the discussion until that individual has a sense of optimism that they can get the job done. The gift you get in return is seeing the positive outcomes that are a result of conversations that are as supportive as you've always intended them to be.

Questions to Guide Your Journey

1. What do your people hear when you give direction—Stop or Go?

2. How are you building confidence with every conversation?

3. What message is your tone and non-verbal communication sending when you ask a question?

Flash-Forward

When Santino was nine, he said something to me that made me feel both proud and humbled. It was a Saturday afternoon, and we were hanging out at home when I came upstairs and saw a big stack of Pokémon cards and a pile of Legos in the hallway. They were scattered everywhere. He had stepped away for a moment to go to the playroom to get more Legos. I kicked into Grumpy Dad mode when I saw the mess. I was probably hungry. I said, "Santino, don't scatter your stuff everywhere like that. We have to walk through here!"

He looked right up at me and said, "Then can you tell me where I can do it? 'Cause I'm trying to build this cool house out of Pokémon cards and Legos and it keeps falling down." Touché, little man. Thanks for keeping Dad in check.

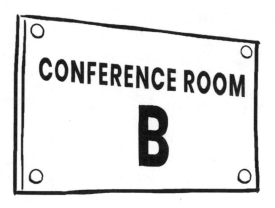

Chapter 9

The Meeting

Having tough conversations was a big part of our culture at PG, and I considered it "permission to play": that is, all part of the norm for how my team behaved. They worked through conflicts openly and without resentment toward each other. My leaders had no problem challenging each other—there was strong peer accountability between them. But even though they teased me about the vein that protruded from the middle of my forehead when I was heated, I hadn't put together that these same courageous and resilient people, unafraid to be honest with one another, were terrified of provoking a reaction from me.

It took a catastrophic meeting to wake me up to that reality. We were huddled in a conference room after we'd had been going back and forth for months about a big financial bet that wouldn't show a return for years. We agreed the opportunity was obvious and demand would continue, but the leader who would live with the consequences felt he and I were miles apart on how we should execute. He voiced his concern, but he thought the CFO and I weren't listening and implied that we didn't trust his ability.

When I spoke up to disagree, sharing my perspective in response, my CFO suddenly exploded at the leader I had challenged. "Why don't you tell him he's wrong? You've already told me. Bobby couldn't be more open to the feedback. Who cares if he gets pissed? We know he's going to get pissed off. He's asking us to tell him when he's wrong."

Every person in the room turned to look at me, waiting for a reaction. I froze, stricken by hearing the truth. I don't know if I was more embarrassed or ashamed by how afraid they were to speak up. I flashed back to episodes when I'd reacted as my CFO described. I could still recall their guarded faces, the same ones I was looking at now. *"I've been muzzling the team I most trust."* A knot formed in my gut, but I also had my finger on the trigger of my opinion. I'm very comfortable with silence (something I inherited from my dad), so I forced it a bit longer than usual as I calmed down.

"Is it true? Are you afraid to tell me?"

The leader I had challenged looked at me. "I'm not afraid of you, but when you get mad, we know it's time to drop it."

All I heard was, "Yes."

The Gift: Speak from the Heart

The meeting ended. I apologized to the team. As I left the room, my mind reeled. From day one, I encouraged my leaders to be painfully transparent with me. Why had no one spoken up sooner? How long had this been going on? I believe the front lines of the company have the most information and should therefore have the loudest voice.

The growth of any company is crippled without honest feedback. I could only imagine how my behavior had prevented ideas from bubbling up from the trenches for years.

I made the mistake of assuming people would speak their minds and tell me when I was wrong. That was easy for me to think; I was at the top of the food chain. Besides, the message was hypocritical anyway, because I also had held back.

The organizations in my past, including the Army, weren't all that interested in my opinions. We've all had "that boss"—the one who tells you they want feedback and then blasts you when you muster up the courage to say something. When I started PG, I was determined to do better. But even though I didn't want to be that boss, I seemed to have developed amnesia about what it was like to be on the other side.

While disappointed, I was lucky that the truth had surfaced. I believe great leaders must lean into the tension these types of conversations expose. Most leaders intuitively want their people to be open and honest about their views. We want to know what holds them back and when they are afraid.

The fear is most apparent when people disagree with the leader. We've all been in that situation, when we get that feeling in our heart telling us to say something. And yet we don't. Often we hold back or dilute our response. Why? We're afraid of the leader's reaction (to say nothing of everyone else in the meeting) if we speak from the heart. We allow our thoughts to spiral when we think about sharing something contrary or difficult. *"If I speak up, no one will believe me." "If I don't go along with the group, I'll be demoted." "I'm the only woman or person of color on this project. If I disagree with the majority, they won't work with me again." "If I contradict my boss, I'll be fired."* These are real fears. The risks aren't imaginary. They happen every day in businesses across the country.

As leaders, we aim to diminish or eliminate this kind of fear. Our reflexive response is to deliver a soothing message, something that doesn't intimidate. We hope for an environment where people know it's safe to speak freely and say anything on their minds in a respectful manner. When your team feels understood, they speak up.

Shari Harley writes in her book, *How to Say Anything to Anyone*, that human beings are hardwired to defend themselves when receiving negative feedback. I had read her book before, but I reread it in light of those recent events with a different set of eyes. When my team attempted to challenge me, I typically defended myself in a heated manner. It didn't matter how much I encouraged people to speak up; it wasn't going to happen if I was out of control.

Harley recommends that leaders acknowledge the person who voices an opposing opinion or offers a new idea with a simple "Thank you for saying that." Skeptical of anything so basic, I doubted that an intractable issue could be remedied with a courteous response. Could just expressing appreciation really make a difference?

But the more I thanked my team and focused on calming my reactions, the more transparent they became. They rewarded me with the gift of challenging me, making me a better leader. I expanded on the opportunities their honesty provided and learned to better understand their fear. I asked open-ended questions and in return shared similar tense moments when I'd been fearful of expressing my ideas.

When challenged, we all know how hard it is to not snap back, to not try to win, or insist on being right. Let's face it: leaders have their own fears to deal with. We don't want to appear weak. But when you respond defensively as a leader, you make things more difficult for everyone, especially yourself. Your people carry the truth you need to hear in their hearts. One of the best compliments a leader will ever receive is to be told by their team that they are wrong.

So often in these situations, we bring the right intention but the wrong view. You can't erase or control another's fear, or even your own. Stop trying. Instead, we need to walk right into the fear together and make it an opportunity to build trust—the most valuable currency you have as a leader.

Questions to Guide
Your Journey

1. When was the last time your team told you that you were wrong?

2. How do you respond when someone shares constructive feedback with you?

3. How do you thank your people for their bravery when they speak up?

Flash-Forward

Our meetings at PG are very different now. I start
our meetings with either good news or a gratitude
exercise. This opens our hearts. My team leans into
candor and healthy tension even more, and this
creates more safety for them to speak freely. I'm still
imperfect, but now it's very common for someone
on the team to make a wisecrack after we discuss
a sensitive topic. "Oh, oh . . . here comes the vein
in Bobby's forehead!" Then they burst into laughter
and tease me about how they could see my blood
boiling in past years concerning similar topics.
I take it in stride—I earned it with my behavior
back then. That said, I'm smiling now, and I
celebrate the safety it creates when I'm willing
to laugh at myself.

Part Three

Choose Your Impact

Hiking with the Kids
Go off the Beaten Path

Desert Shower
More Is Not the Answer

Rainier
Not Everyone Will Summit

The Toy Pile
Work as One

Chapter 10

Hiking with the Kids

These days, I hike with my three kids every chance I get. We scramble along the wooded trails until I call out, "Where do Herreras go?" They shout their response in unison: "We go off the beaten path!"

That's the cue to leave the well-worn path we're on and strike out to find adventure. The kids keep the trail in sight as they wander off to discover new plants, insects, or animal tracks. They collect moss, climb trees, build forts, and cover themselves in dirt. While they explore, I clear a spot nearby, and soon we're lying down side by side to play a game of I Spy. We point out everything we notice with our backs on the hard ground and our eyes gazing skyward. We look for imaginary forest people, the ones we read about in fairy tales, believing they have recently passed this way too.

I'm drawn to exploration, particularly in the mountains. One day in the summer of 2009 as I prepared for a climb, I took a training hike up Mailbox Peak, a steep trail cut by the boots of avid hikers. The punishing elevation gain coupled with the weight of my pack made for a torturous day.

As I hiked, I thought about the themes that connected my time in the Army and mountain climbing. I realized they both used symbols and stories to promote courage. The military uses rigorous routine, awards prestigious medals, and holds elaborate ceremonies to cultivate strength, unit cohesion, and honor. The climbing community has their own vocabulary, levels of mastery, and celebratory tales of those who complete the Seven Summits or other tests of endurance and determination. The symbols, ceremonies, and traditions create lore that inspires others.

By the time I made it to the top of Mailbox Peak, I was both exhausted and energized. I wanted to instill my passion for exploration within the culture at PG. Gazing at the view spread out below me, I decided that to inspire people, I would incorporate symbols and traditions that would embed the importance of challenge and discovery within the company.

When I'm with the kids, without fail, other hikers stop to ask if we're okay. The rule-bound sort feels obliged to inform us we shouldn't be off the path. We're polite and wave at these fellow travelers, but we never stop having fun. Once in a while, other daring kids ask to join us, and they become part of our adventure. Welcomed with open (if grubby) arms, the kids quickly bond, and together they investigate every new and unknown thing that can only be found by leaving the trail and following their nose.

By the time we return to the parking lot, my intrepid explorers are spent, starving, filthy, and joyful. The best part of the day is listening to them later, telling their mom everything they never would have seen or known if they hadn't gone off the beaten path.

I'm convinced we must all remain explorers. Whether it's in family or business, we need to continually venture into new and untested territory, primed for adventure and discovery.

The Gift:
Go off the Beaten Path

I used to assume that anyone I selected to join my team would watch me go off the beaten path once or twice and follow my lead. A few did, but most didn't.

I understood their reluctance, even though it frustrated me. Few leaders that I'd worked for embraced any sort of innovation or venturing off course. Most people I hired had worked in similar situations, and it showed in the way they sought my validation or asked permission to change a process or improve a task. This drove me nuts as I struggled to underscore the necessity of risk-taking to drive innovation. I wanted people to introduce better and more efficient ways of working, but I was up against a barrier that seemed hardwired in people's brains.

I was determined to build a culture where people felt safe to try new things—even if it meant going against the grain. I overdid it by telling countless stories about my attempts to innovate in my previous jobs. Most of my tales ended with a compliance manager redirecting me back to the well-worn path. Because of those disheartening experiences, I applauded anything large or small that involved doing something novel. But none of these efforts were producing results fast enough for me.

To make innovation a living intention within the company, I started using the term "insultant," which I first learned from Dr. Ichak Adizes, who writes about corporate life cycles. The idea is for every person at PG to "consult from the inside." I want everyone to view innovation as an everyday occurrence rather than an aberration from the daily work we accomplish.

To help encourage this mindset, I repeatedly ask, "Tell me about something that annoys you. What should we be doing differently?" Without fail, the conversation turns to something that frustrates the team member. It might be a company inefficiency, a constraint that hinders better customer service, or an issue with their current role. The question prompts open discussion about what needs to change and how.

The other part of the conversation is to ask, "What annoys our customers?" Dennis Snow, an author, friend, and mentor, introduced me to the concept of "service mapping." The exercise looks at every process through the customer's experience rather than our company. By flipping the lens, it helps to identify what the customer sees and encounters in every interaction with our organization. The service mapping review opened our eyes to "pain points" that annoyed our customers, and it ignited awareness about nonessential steps to remove, making things easier for the client and in turn streamlining the delivery of our services.

The Army had taught me the power of after-action reviews, and I adapted them for PG. The structured review (or "debrief") was convened following training exercises to candidly assess what happened, why, and how to improve the next exercise or mission. Even in the military's strict hierarchy, debriefs prompted questions, open dialogue, and procedural changes. As a leader, I wanted to introduce a routine that encouraged a review after any significant company event to spark a reflective conversation and make our performance stronger the next time around. In my experience, someone in the debrief will inevitably say, "What if we did this?" That's the one-liner that opens an innovative dialogue. People around the table begin to toss out new thoughts, reacting to and refining the idea that's been proposed.

Any process left in place too long can become inefficient. I introduced the phrase "resetting the broken arm" to remind us to break things in order to make them better. When a process or routine settles for too long, it's time to break it again. There are few instances in business where a way of doing something continues to derive the same benefit over a protracted time period. This kind of innovation is about refreshing the things you do well and reaping the rewards of continuous improvement. You and your people must learn to strike a balance between high-performance continuity and disrupting any procedure that has gone unquestioned for too long.

Leaders tend to identify struggle and naturally look for innovation. Once you establish the idea that you are expecting innovation to improve even the smallest annoyance, every pain point in the company becomes an opportunity for exploration and improvement. At PG, people must demonstrate the courage to challenge the company status quo. To shake up the routine and refine our methods, people have transformed services we offer, while others have devised tweaks to enhance the employee experience. People understand it's safe to explore, challenge, and investigate. They no longer wait for permission but are aware that the greatest career hazard at PG is to plod along the well-traveled trail.

We've introduced significant incentives to reward innovation, including all-expenses-paid vacations for top innovators. There are customs and traditions that remind people that daily exploration is mandatory, not optional. The stories of our exploits have multiplied, and the lore has grown. All of these are powerful tools when it comes to changing the limiting mindset most companies engender. In exchange, I've been given a gift that benefits everyone on the team while helping the company remain competitive for years to come. Leaders, whatever beaten path you're on, think instead about pursuing what lies undiscovered off the trail. It won't go as planned, but you've got to ask yourself . . . what's the best that could happen?

Questions to Guide Your Journey

1. How are you asking people for their input and ideas?

2. How do your leaders mine for new ideas in their interactions and meetings?

3. What routines, rituals, and rewards have you built into your culture to encourage risk-taking?

Flash-Forward

On a rainy afternoon in 2017, my boys and I
were hiking the shorter and steeper trail of Poo Poo
Point on West Tiger Mountain near Issaquah,
Washington. As we approached a vista point near
the top, a group of hikers were resting and enjoying
some lunch. We stopped to rest too. The trail
continued to the right—but off to the left,
there was a clearing that looked like it may have
connected to the trail further up. We took it. A
short while later, I noticed the hikers we'd passed
had followed us. My boys started pointing out
new discoveries they hadn't seen before, and
the other hikers soon did the same. One finally
said to me, "I've been on this hike many times
and have always wondered where this would take
you. How often do you take this route?"

"It's our first time!"

He laughed, then said, "I guess I just needed
to see someone go off the trail."

Chapter 11

Desert Shower

While I was in the Army, I spent six to eight weeks every year in the Mojave Desert, where temperatures often surpassed 120 degrees. The Mojave Desert is home to the Fort Irwin National Training Center, where I and my fellow field artillery soldiers were on the move day and night, dressed in full gear in conditions that approximated what we would encounter in the Middle East. We all quickly ripened under the unrelenting sun and soon smelled worse than a horde of zombies fresh from their graves. Throughout our training at Fort Irwin, we were only allowed to bathe every two weeks or so.

On my first trip to the Mojave Desert, my fantasy of enjoying a long, hot shower after fourteen days of training existed only until I saw that the shower station made the set of *M*A*S*H* seem like a luxury hotel. It had the effect of looking like you were showering in a barrel, with your legs and head exposed, but the true disappointment was seeing the two-gallon bucket with a shower head attached to the bottom that hung over the stall. My heart sinking, I knew I'd need to refill it at least ten times to get clean.

Standing on a wooden pallet with a tarp configured to act as a stall, things got worse. The soldier responsible for distributing the water told me that what was in the bucket was all the water I'd get. In fact, he asked me not to use it all so there would be more for the next crew.

He offered these instructions: "Turn the shower head, and it will begin to slowly drip. Start lathering immediately from your head to your feet and let the drip do the work."

Completely unconvinced by the directions, I entertained the idea of scooping water directly from the bucket and washing however I wanted. I briefly imagined this was some kind of prank and the joke would soon be up, followed by a good laugh and a real shower. In the end, I give up on my errant thoughts and did what I was told.

I turned the shower head and started the drip. To my ears, the bar soap scraping over the stubble on my head sounded like steel wool rubbing across a thick-skinned gourd. I moved at warp speed, believing the water would be gone in an instant. As I continued to lather from the top down, it didn't take long until I felt the drips making their way down my body. As the water continued to work its way toward my feet, the drops seemed to increase from a trickle to a stream. I soon quit worrying about the water and focused on getting clean. By the time I reached my toes, the persistent drip of the soapy water had done most of the work for me.

In twenty minutes I was clean as a whistle. I checked the water bucket and, to my amazement, found it was still half full. Exiting the stall to make way for the next soldier, I was amazed once more by the power of scarcity.

— — —

The Gift:
More Is Not the Answer

Every day, leaders contend with the question of time versus money. During the early years at PG, survival depended on our ingenuity and a bare-bones operation to beat our competitors. As the company became more successful, the temptation was to add more resources at the first sign of difficulty. After all, isn't the point of success to outgrow the uncomfortable constraints of hard times? As time went on, I noticed that when leaders at PG became overwhelmed, particularly when they were handed more responsibility, they typically asked for more people, more tools, and more money to meet the demands in front of them. I struggled to give my leaders perspective on how to manage growing challenges successfully while using the fewest resources possible.

When I was growing up in New Mexico, doing more with less was a way of life. Like every impoverished family, more was never an option for us. The attitude embedded in my DNA from childhood was reinforced by the Army. In the military, resourcefulness is baked into the design of any operation. We would assess everything available to us in the moment and adjust accordingly to meet our objective. Our greatest assets were time, energy, and a laser-like focus on completing the mission.

Soldiers are trained to pick the best path and give it a disproportionate amount of their energy. In business, whether we're early-stage entrepreneurs or the leaders of large organizations, the tendency is to throw more money at our problems in some form or fashion. But the truth is that we're more effective when we manage with less because constraints force us to stay focused and be creative.

In the competition between time and money, time is rarely viewed as the more important commodity. I learned a lot about time when the company went through a stressful period of rapid growth. One night, I wrote down every problem I was trying to solve and any issue that bothered me. An hour later, I felt relieved to have flushed everything out of my mind and onto the four pages I had filled. Though I now had a "Flush List," it took me a while to make sense of it all.

If I ask someone who has the most influence in a company, I'm commonly told that it's the person with the most important role or the greatest expertise. In my opinion, influence in a company is defined by the time horizon in which you think. In practice, do people with the most influence invest their time in day-to-day problems or "big bet" opportunities? It's the big bets, of course, and those key issues take time to solve. As I reviewed my Flush List, I realized how little I had been investing in problems and opportunities that required a lot of time. To change that situation, I placed every issue or task on my list in one of the following three columns, depending on the time horizon each one needed to be resolved:

- Day to day
- Six to eighteen months
- Two to three years

When I perform this exercise with leaders, they feel as relieved as I did to see everything on the page. But the real test comes when they open their calendar and discover what percentage of their time is invested in solving problems in each particular bucket. They quickly realize their time is being eaten up by the immediate tasks that too many leaders get pulled into, while their work on big bets that in time will make the greatest impact on the business is ignored.

Completing this exercise proves to my leaders that we have more time than we think. To optimize our time use, leaders are required to focus on a few top priorities, applying energy over time. Less important responsibilities are delegated to others. We continually refer to business opportunities in terms of their time horizon. How long will they take to be realized, and how much energy needs to be consistently applied over that period?

Building resourcefulness is about challenging the way you're currently doing things. It starts at the top with the CEO. To me, the E in the acronym stands for "Edit." It's the CEO's job to edit, or eliminate, all unnecessary or redundant work, making things easier for their people. Resourcefulness is not only about the best application of the tools you have but also about eliminating anything that creates a burden.

Without realizing it, your customers may be challenging you to creatively edit as well. For example, when our customers tell us they want more, what I believe they are telling us is they want to do less. They are saying, "I want it to be simpler and easier for me to work with you."

This request is an incredible opportunity for leaders to gain loyalty from customers and engage their team. We must look for places to edit and then do so in ways that benefit everyone. Pick a process in your organization and challenge the team responsible for it to make the procedure easier on the customer by removing two of the steps. Easy to do? Heck no! It requires looking at the whole picture and applying time, energy, and creativity to improve the customer experience.

When my leaders ask for more resources, I respond with a question that instantly changes their focus. "On a scale of one to ten, how well are you doing with everything currently available to you?" As I continue to ask follow-up questions, we assess all of the leader's responsibilities. This never fails to uncover countless ways to raise the average performance of their team. Resourcefulness in this case amounts to incremental changes and small shifts that allow our teams to function as close to full capacity as humanly possible.

The point of this assessment is also to consider how and when it might be appropriate to add more. I refer to this as the "gray conversation." Rather than saying yes or no to the request for more, I ask my leaders to get comfortable with the gray area in between. It means stretching their teams, editing their processes, and applying energy and creativity to every problem. And while they are raising the average performance of the team, we can open a dialogue about how and when more might be needed. By working in the gray zone, my leaders and I always find that we have more resources than we think, and when we do need more, it's always less than anyone expected.

The essence of resourcefulness is courage. Leaders feel like heroes when they say yes to more. While seeking that ego boost is natural, it's misguided. Leaders are required to make hard choices by assessing exactly when to say yes and no. Courage is knowing you can do more with less.

Leaders are naturally ambitious, and they are generally as eager to have more as the people they lead. But a word of caution to leaders who may misinterpret this lesson: maintaining your ambitions while carefully managing resources is not an excuse for being cheap or abusing the people in your company. On the contrary, the gift of choosing resourcefulness isn't merely to run a leaner, more profitable company; it's about finding balance. Resourcefulness has taught me to be grateful, appreciating everything I have while quieting my own ravenous appetite for more.

— — —

Questions to Guide
Your Journey

1. Do you know all the problems you must solve
and all their deadlines?

2. Do you know all the problems your leaders
believe they must solve and their deadlines?

3. What responsibility can I delegate to
someone else?

Flash-Forward

I recently promoted a leader to my executive team. PG was performing fairly well, but we knew there was more potential if he took responsibility for a segment of the business I had overseen for years.

As we discussed his new role, he requested that we double the size of the team by the end of the year. He wanted more people and more tools to get the job done.

"Are you sure?" I asked.

"Yes."

I asked him to rate the team's performance. He quickly gave his answer—five on a scale of ten.

Does that team average of five get to a seven or an eight if you add more people? Is more really the answer?

We both knew adding to the team would immediately drive the average lower.

"Get the team average up to seven, and then let's talk about the resources you're asking for," I said.

That year he guided his team to our best performance in a decade. When I reminded him of our initial conversation, he smiled and admitted how nervous he had been to ask for more.

It takes a shift in perspective to do more with less. Leaders must make sure that every person and asset is functioning at their best before committing resources that may be better used for some other purpose.

Chapter 12

Rainier

When we moved to Seattle in 2008, I enjoyed amazing views of Mount Rainier on my daily commute as I crossed Lake Washington. I've been captivated by mountains since I was sixteen, finding them to be beautiful and therapeutic. The challenge of summiting a peak intrigued me. Not long after our move to the Pacific Northwest, I signed up to climb Mount Rainier the following summer, much to my pregnant wife's chagrin. Given what little free time I had away from the business, she had other ideas about what I could be doing.

I started training the following April in the pre-dawn hours. Santino was an infant.

I followed my training regimen as closely as I could, given the circumstances at home, and worked to prepare for the August climb. Four months later, I was tired but in the best shape I'd been in since I was in the Army.

As the date approached, my buddy Britt flew in. I'd convinced him to train and come with me. On the day of the climb, we headed to the mountain and met the guides and the other ten climbers in our group. Every group starts from Camp Muir at an elevation of 10,000 feet and makes the 4,400-foot climb to the summit. You make your summit bid by starting late at night, reaching the summit by morning, and returning back to Camp Muir the same day.

That evening we covered the details of the route while the guides inspected our equipment. We departed at 1:00 a.m. without having slept a wink. Adrenaline and nerves made us all jittery. We just wanted to get going and get it over with.

A couple hours in, halfway up Disappointment Cleaver, four climbers quit; two guides escorted them back to Camp Muir. A guide informed us that this was the point at which 90% of climbers fail or give up. It's not only steep, sandy, and rocky, but oxygen is scarce. It tests your endurance and your will when you realize it's only halfway to the summit.

Ascending the Cleaver, we had two more segments to reach the summit by sunrise. We lost another climber to altitude sickness. The guide told us if one more climber dropped out, we'd all have to return to Camp Muir. Those of us who remained stiffened our resolve. None of us wanted to be the one that turned the whole party around.

The storm hit on the final run to the top. We had been warned it was coming. The orange sun and black clouds were stunning and troublesome. Blistering wind and cold grew fiercer with every step. It felt as though someone was pulling us backwards with a rope. The air was so thin I felt like I was breathing through a straw.

As we reached the summit just before 7:00 a.m., icicles formed on our gear. We celebrated and hurriedly snapped photos. I posed with the PG flag I'd made and got the picture I wanted to share. The storm worsened, so given the conditions, we skipped the hour of rest usually allowed before descending.

Only seven of twelve climbers made it that day. Two quit, two got altitude sickness, and one injured her knee. I asked the guide how many times he'd had everyone in their group reach the summit. He told me, "I can't recall a climb when everyone made it to the top. It's possible, I guess, but it seems like something always happens."

- - -

The Gift:
Not Everyone Will Summit

I used to invest a great deal of time and effort in building my teams and consequently put extreme pressure on myself to keep them together. When someone left the company, I beat myself up for days. It's hard when you've put time and energy into someone who then decides to leave. This feeling of loss is shared by most leaders who care deeply about their people.

When I pause now and think about my perspective in earlier years, I shake my head at how ridiculous it was to think I could retain my entire team as I built the company. We know most things work out differently than we plan. Why shouldn't that apply to our employees? It's universal for everyone.

The Mount Rainier climb provided a new way to metaphorically illustrate how I understood the company. In my view, the climb is continuous and never ending. There is always another summit. It's how I remain aware of the fact that PG has to continually improve to remain a competitive business. Everyone at PG is a climber on the ascent toward personal and professional growth. As teams we are stronger, go further, and accomplish more than we ever could alone. There is no actual summit in business. There are peaks and valleys—the business cycles we endure, the victories and pain points within an organization—that we experience as highs and lows. And yet as long as our doors remain open, there is no final endpoint, only new challenges, problems, innovations, and solutions.

This metaphor also helped me realize a few key things about the team you start with, those who leave in pursuit of other ventures, and those who continue the climb. It's important to realize we are all climbing our own mountains. Everyone you hire started their career climb before you met them, and they will likely continue climbing for a long time after their tenure with your company is over. All of us are working within our own set of constraints, goals, and unexpected life events that shape our journey.

We all climb for different reasons, so it's important to honor people's dreams. Most of us aspire to multiple life goals and are committed to relationships that demand flexibility and sacrifice. The reasons people stay or leave may be tied to a more far-flung and adventurous path than any single role within a company can accommodate.

Your job as a leader is to encourage the growth of your people and to appreciate their particular contributions to the ongoing climb of the company. Regardless of when a person chooses to strike out on a different course, celebrate your time together. Life is a sequence of intersections, shared efforts, and differing goals. I've seen lives change in an instant, and I often say that we're all just one phone call away from being on our knees. Taking this view makes me grateful for my team while we are together and helps me continue to appreciate a climber after we've parted ways.

After I shifted my perspective, I could worry less—but not care less—about losing someone on my team. Like the guide on the mountain had told me, something always happens. When someone on the team leaves the company, I look for the gift by understanding the reason behind the departure. If I can fix anything internal to PG and help everyone that remains on the team, I make the change. If I can't, we press ahead, knowing a new team member will join us and bring their own unique gifts to contribute. I feel liberated by a mindset that keeps me focused and present with the team I have with me on the mountain, rather than being disheartened by those who have left to scale peaks of their own.

I have never lost the desire to keep the team I've built. I've been fortunate to have done well on that score. Adopting this rationale does not mean it's acceptable to lose good people. The reality is you will always face attrition for many reasons you can't control. But as a leader you must not allow it to distract you from the main goal: guiding your teams as best you can for as far as they are willing to climb with you. And when they choose a different journey, don't stop cherishing the time in which you shared the same story.

It's helpful to think of people who move on to follow other pursuits as the alumni of your company. Don't write them off. Maintain the connection and keep them in your network. Former team members may still make surprising contributions to your business in the future. Though I haven't been perfect in applying this more generous perspective, my appreciation and respect for all the great people that have climbed with me continues to grow. Their successes deserve to be acknowledged as much as those who are still part of the PG climb.

The photo I took at the summit of Mount Rainier as I raised the PG flag is a symbol of the gift I received. I learned to accept attrition with mindfulness of what I can control and faith that the people who leave are fulfilling the climb intended for them.

Questions to Guide
Your Journey

1. What perspective do you have when you lose someone on your team?

2. How are you applying these lessons to keep you more present with your current team?

3. How do you help people that chose to leave your team?

Flash-Forward

Paul, who was part of the PG team for six years, chose to leave the company and pursue a different path. But it wasn't the end of our climb, so I asked Paul to tell his side of the story. The following is his perspective:

"The choice to leave PG was a difficult one. During my six years at PG, I built lifelong friendships. That foundation allowed me to maintain a strong connection with Bobby. I always envisioned working with great teams, moving up the ladder, and having an impact within the organization. After my tenure with PG, where I worked with great mentors and leaders, it made it very difficult to work with other organizations that didn't hold the values I'd become accustomed to.

I had always tossed around the idea of owning a company, but I never thought it would happen. I came to realize Bobby's unselfish mentorship had given me the skills, confidence, and courage to begin the entrepreneur's journey.

Throughout my three years in business, Bobby has been a significant mentor, coach, and friend. When I tell others that my former CEO is one of my biggest supporters, most people are in disbelief. Investing your life savings in a start-up in your mid-thirties is scary. The best thing to have around you are coaches and mentors to help you maneuver avoidable blind spots. Bobby has provided a level of accountability, candor, and transparency over the years that I deeply appreciate. To express my thanks, I do my best to conscientiously apply what he has taken the time to teach me."

Chapter 13

The Toy Pile

One evening, I came home to . . . nothing. No little feet beating a path to the door, no one to greet me, no happy voices competing for my attention. Peeking around the corner of the mud room, I finally got a "Hi, Dada!" but failed miserably to redirect the focus of any of my children.

A little bummed about being ignored, I grabbed a beer and got caught up on Roslyn's day as I watched my daughter, Sofia. She was consumed by the task of stacking her toys into an enormous mound in the middle of the living room. Building a toy tower was a game she had played before. The question was how long she could hold her own. Within minutes the toy tower had achieved sufficient scale to attract the attention of her older brothers, Santino and Griffith, who had been playing a game of their own. Abandoning what they had been doing, they tried to muscle in on Sofia's domain.

Santino immediately tried to bull rush her pile and add a toy to the stack. Screaming "No!" my daughter stood her ground. Grif got shut down with another "No!" when he attempted the same. Sofia wasn't about to be overpowered by the boys. Quickly deciding to double-team her, the brothers swooped in on the tower like velociraptors from Jurassic Park, coming from all angles. But my rebel girl didn't budge. Standing in front of the tower with her arms extended, she yelled, "No! It's my pile!"

The boys persisted, but after a few unsuccessful flybys, Santino took a new approach. He ran to the playroom and then returned with a toy in each hand.

"Look Sofia, two of your toys. Where do they go?" She immediately softened.

"Oh! Right here! And here!" She took one from his hand and placed it on top of the stack and then pointed for him to place the other one halfway up. Grif caught on, made his own trip to the playroom, and got the same go-ahead response when he returned.

As the new game continued, the boys became frantic as they ran for more of Sofia's toys.

"Where do you want me to put these?"

"Right here!" Sofia, the happy architect of her tower, relished bossing around her big brothers.

A bit shocked at the turn of events, I truly enjoyed the moment. Watching it unfold, I couldn't help but wonder how amazing would it be if we all acted like this.

The Gift:
Work as One

Everyone at PG was suddenly on edge. Due to a strategic error, our largest customer was heading for a downturn, creating a major ripple effect for us. As we monitored the impact, it quickly became clear that things were going to be worse than anticipated. During the routine set of meetings with my team, I noticed an insane amount of energy was being spent on rework and redundancy spread across our teams. Our leaders were frustrated and overwhelmed. Although our company philosophy encouraged making mistakes in order to innovate and grow, we agreed we were making too many now. We all know repeating the same mistake over and over is the definition of crazy.

I dove in to figure out why we were out of sync. As I met with PG leaders, I identified a common thread. Everyone had a different answer when I asked them to name our most important priority. I started to understand that I hadn't made our top objective crystal clear for everyone. Lack of clarity had created silos across our ecosystem. People were not only building but also fiercely protecting their own towers.

As leaders, we've been taught to set priorities for our organization. We all want to believe we're better than most at pinpointing targets and messaging priorities. But using a traditional approach goes something like this: Every year you roll out the top three priorities with a bunch of metrics attached to each. Some years there are as many as five priorities, though they're still in line with parameters suggested by the experts.

In addition, if you're like me, you ask leaders to set additional priorities for their branch or division. And then everyone on their team does the same for their own teams. Now pause and do the math. How many different priorities is every individual executing? The further the teams are from the hub of the wheel, where you sit, the more complex the work initiatives become as people decide what's most critical among three or more sets of differing priorities. This is how silos are erected and how communication breaks down. Frustration and defensiveness come to rule at every level. Competing mandates ensure that no one works together. Now add a business setback or a full-blown crisis, and what do you have on your hands?

As leaders, we must unite our teams and eliminate the silos and infighting we unintentionally encourage. Having long been a student of Patrick Lencioni's work, I can recommend one of his leadership fables. *Silos, Politics, and Turf Wars* is a helpful book for organizations determined to improve the working relationships between departments and create a better experience for everyone. In reading about his thematic goal model, I found hope that I could pull us through our struggle and identify the gift it was hiding.

I educated the entire team on the thematic goal methodology. Using this method, I crafted a single rally cry for a specified time period. For it to be effective, the organization has to come to agreement and support the call.

We held a meeting in Chicago to candidly assess our current situation and answer the question, "What's most important right now?" The session was brutal, and I felt horrible. Silos had bred rigid defenses. I saw firsthand how badly people wanted to work together and how that intention was thwarted by the barriers erected by differing priorities among teams. After two days of revealing and candid discussions, we framed the first rally cry for the organization. We left knowing exactly what was most important for the next nine months. Back at the office, we communicated the rally cry and got every person aligned with it. I fell on my sword and owned my part in the proliferation of towers I had never wanted people to build.

We all worked toward one goal for the next nine months. As the teams felt the change, they took it upon themselves to devise and implement better ways of working together. The teams were liberated by knowing what mattered most. As a leader, I saw what a difference it made to take responsibility for setting priorities and offering clear goals while establishing a collaborative environment for everyone.

We can't always control the situations in which we find ourselves, but we do get to choose how we respond, how we guide our teams, and where we invest our time and energy. I understand how hard it is to unite a team. We allow ourselves to pursue several priorities, convinced they are all urgent and significant and that we can successfully pursue them all at once. But it's far more productive to slow down and ask a clear and direct question: "What's our single most important priority?"

Demanding that our people do more is not the answer but rather an expectation that leaves everyone irritated and pushing back on each other. If you want to build anything worthwhile, do it together. The gift will be not just how much more you achieve but also how much fun you have tearing down your silos and building a united organization.

Questions to Guide
Your Journey

1. Does your company know the single biggest problem you must solve together?

2. How are you encouraging your leaders to work as one?

3. How are your leaders encouraging their teams to find better ways to work together?

Flash-Forward

When I turn on my computer in the morning,
I see one of my favorite pictures in the world.
It's a picture of my three kids playing in a sandbox,
taken about a year after the toy pile story occurred.
In the picture, my daughter is standing in the
middle of the sandbox, and she is looking down
at her bare little feet. Her brothers are kneeling
down by her side—they are burying her feet
with sand. The words on the purple T-shirt my
daughter is wearing say, "Life Is Better Together."

- - -

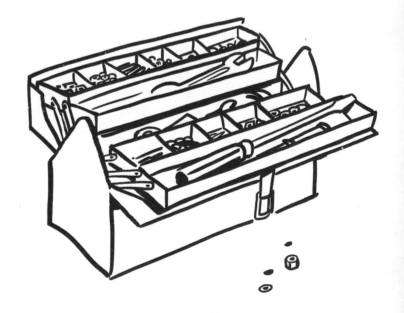

Chapter 14

Become a Student of Struggle

Early in the morning following my eighteenth birthday, I waited outside the gym at my school for the Army recruiter. My parents didn't know, but I had told a short list of people that I was planning to enlist. They were all sworn to secrecy. We drove forty-four miles to Hobbs, New Mexico, where I boarded a bus to the Military Entrance Processing Station in Amarillo, Texas.

The following day, I was sworn into the Army, and the recruiter dropped me off at my house in the early evening. I feared my parents knew I hadn't stayed at my best friend's the night prior, and I knew my dad would be furious. I was the first of my siblings to take the oath, and we all knew you didn't dare test my dad's authority. I walked in the front door, and my dad was sitting at the head of the table. He immediately stood when I walked in, and I could tell by his body language that he was not happy. I had to act fast. Walking in my direction, he began peppering me with questions about where I stayed the prior evening. I said nothing and tossed the folder with my Army enlistment paperwork on the table.

I then told him in Spanish, "I joined the Army, Papa."

His body language immediately softened and he silently stared.

"Do you know what you're doing?" he asked.

I responded, "Yes. I'm completing your dream, Papa."

Tears welled up in his eyes as he turned around and walked toward the window in the kitchen. Looking out, his shoulders shook a bit, and he raised his hand to wipe the tears away. He waited a moment before he walked out the back door. I looked over at my mom, who had tears on her face. It was the second time in my life I'd seen my dad cry.

Early in my life, he shared the story of his dream as a teenager to join *las Fuerzas Armadas de México*—the Mexican Army. Joining the military was the only way he saw then to break the generational cycle of poverty that had been passed down in the family. His dream had been derailed by severe family hardships as he was coming of age, and he was unable to enlist. He would have to find another way out while his struggles continued to shape him for many years.

Something in his tone when I heard the story made my heart ache. I recall thinking how I would do anything to mend that hole. The year following the bus story, I vividly remember realizing that perhaps I could help him. The military recruiters had started visiting more often, and the more I sat with them, the more I wanted to serve.

That last week when I sat with my dad before he passed, he told me how much it had meant that I had done that for him. We never discussed it that evening after I told him I had enlisted. This time, when I heard the story, we both wept. His tone was different. He told me he was proud of me and that I had filled the hole in his heart.

We all have someone who has struggled through hard choices so that our own may be different—better, perhaps. Early on and throughout his life, my dad faced many struggles. He constantly told me stories about the gifts those struggles gave him. When his grandchildren fell down, he would always smile and say, "That's how we learn." I always felt that the least I could do was to show him and my mother how grateful I was by becoming a student of their struggles. Choosing to join the Army was my gift to my dad: I would complete his dream.

Every day when I walk into my office, the first thing I see above the light switch is a picture of my dad's bracero card. It keeps me grounded and focused as I remain a student. That card is my proudest symbol of how struggle has been my teacher.

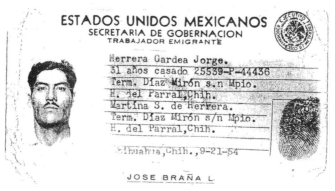

ESTADOS UNIDOS MEXICANOS
SECRETARIA DE GOBERNACION
TRABAJADOR EMIGRANTE

Herrera Gardea Jorge.
31 años casado 25539-P-44436
Term. Díaz Mirón s/n Mpio.
H. del Parral,Chih.
Martina S. de Herrera.
Term. Díaz Mirón s/n Mpio.
H. del Parral,Chih.

Chihuahua,Chih.,9-21-54

JOSE BRAÑA L.

Begin Your Journey

So how do you begin your journey as a student
of struggle?

Start by openly inviting struggle into your life.
Too many people silence or ignore their struggles.
We all struggle, and it will be with us for as long
as we live. You must decide for yourself that struggle
is a good thing, that struggle is a gift.

Once you do, identify what your struggles have
been and reflect deeply on them. As you reflect,
consider how they have helped you become a better
version of who you are today. How have they made
you stronger? More resilient? More compassionate?
The answers to these questions are the powerful gifts
that have shaped your life. Those are the gifts. This
is the work that will help you better understand your
leadership potential and who you are becoming.

From there, you will have the clarity you need to
begin the journey to become the leader you imagine.
Your desire to improve must overrule your need
for comfort. You will have to confront the emotions
that struggle brings up to develop the courage
to share your stories and your gifts. There is an

incredible need in the world for us to learn from one another and help others, to be more compassionate and kind. You must share your gifts of struggle so that we all may become better people.

For aspiring leaders and those of you early in your leadership journey, you'll soon learn that the lessons outlined in these chapters are not a chronological list. There is a lot of ambiguity in leadership. Some of you will want a "how to" checklist. You want the answers to the test. I get it.

There is healthy tension between the lessons I shared in this book. I encourage you to go off the beaten path in Chapter 10, and then Chapter 11 says to trust the process, that less is more. For someone early in their leadership journey, this could be perceived as a mixed message. I understand that it can be confusing. Leadership isn't easy. It's complex, overwhelming, and messy. You're going to have to struggle through situations for yourself, like I did.

But what I can do is encourage you to think of these lessons as an "and" not an "or." Your struggles will be situational and unique to you—identify and study them first, then determine which lesson will best guide you. Sometimes it will be a combination of a few, and the others may not apply. Let your struggles decide. The more you do this, the better you will become at dealing with the ambiguity of becoming a leader.

Let me end with this:

I know you can do it.
You have more potential than you realize.
All Hail the Underdogs!

- - -

Pay It Forward

A Guide for Leaders Using *The Gift of Struggle*

In my experience, the word "leader" can quickly bloom into a big topic. Most people overcomplicate what it means and what it takes to become a great leader. I've come to believe that leadership is about heart—it's about who we are and how we choose to lead. I wrote this book to help leaders who truly want to make a difference in people's lives.

My nephew Luke nailed the essence of the definition. He was applying to run for a position on the student council at his school. The first question in his application was, "In your opinion, what makes a great leader?"

Luke wrote, "A leader is someone willing to help others."

You will notice that I often use the term "aspiring leader" in this book. This is my way of signaling to you that leadership is an infinite journey—there is no final line to cross. We must always be self-evaluating how we serve others. We must also evolve with the times as they change.

As you finish reading the book, here is an important question to consider:

How can you better guide other leaders?

Here are the organizing principles I used in the book, with suggestions about how you can use *The Gift of Struggle* with other leaders.

Part 1:
Who Am I?

Part One is called "Who Am I?"; like any good story, the beginning always sets the tone. It all starts and ends with who you are and what you believe. You must first look inward and lead yourself before you will be great at leading others. This is foundational to any leadership journey. If this foundation isn't strong, you will struggle to build on a life that gives you fulfillment. Most leaders fail to put enough emphasis on this part of their story because it requires a level of vulnerability and courage they are afraid to tap into. I understand. It's also unfortunate. Your willingness to share determines how effectively you will build trust with others. This is where you share your story and what you imagine for your group.

Part 2:
Give > Take

The middle part of a story gets messy as you try to figure out the way you want to lead. The challenge for many leaders is the discomfort and self-doubt that comes with all the mistakes you will make during this part of the journey. You start by owning the part you play in the conflicts and struggles that arise. Leaders are students, always getting better at what they do and working with the people they lead. Better questions expose better answers and more truth. This part of your journey is where you begin building on the strong foundation. You will start to understand the power of compassion and generosity once you get a grip on how you will lead. You ultimately learn that the long way really is the shortcut.

Part 3:
Choose Your Impact

This phase of the journey is all about choice.
The final part of a good story is where things start to come together. Once people know why you lead and how you lead, you must consistently guide them so they can benefit from all the hard lessons you've learned. Not everyone will make it through to the end of the journey. Leaders work especially hard at bringing people together to multiply their potential. Leaders work with their teams to balance priorities and resources to produce results for the team and the organization.

Guides to Help You Learn from Struggle

In Chapter 7, I shared that the best leaders are always learning. Although my hope is that my stories have helped you understand how your struggles will help you, I have often needed more than my desire and my will to get to the gift at the heart of each hardship. Books are the greatest resource that I can recommend to you. Through the years I have placed my best guides on a separate shelf I call "Bible Row." I revisit them frequently. They make me think and ask myself better and bigger questions, guiding me to identify the gifts in my struggles. The following is a short list of some of my favorite leadership books from Bible Row:

The Advantage: Why Organizational Health Trumps Everything Else in Business — Patrick Lencioni

The Speed of Trust: The One Thing that Changes Everything — Stephen M. R. Covey

Start with Why: How Great Leaders Inspire Everyone to Take Action –– Simon Sinek

Great by Choice: Uncertainty, Chaos, and Luck— Why Some Thrive Despite Them All — Jim Collins

Great Leaders Ask Great Questions: Your Foundation for Successful Leadership — John C. Maxwell

For other lists of my favorite books, visit bobby-herrera.com.

Acknowledgments

Every lesson in this book has the strength of my parents. *Mama, tus sacrificios nunca se perdieron en mí. Siempre me siento humilde, agradecido, y orgulloso de todos los regalos que me brindaron tus luchas.*

My Team One: I'm so proud of you. Roslyn, you have always given me your unconditional support. Your love and advice over the years are embedded in all these gifts. "Thank you" isn't enough for how happy you've made me.

My Coconuts—Santino, Griffith, and Sofia, above everything, all I want is to be your All-Pro Dad. *Los amo con todo mi corazon.*

Ed, my brother, best friend, and the other kid on the bus: I love you, brother.

The Circle, your courage and character has always inspired me. You've helped me build something very special for many. I'm grateful to be a part of your story and carry the coin.

Mrs. Roach, my second mom, I love you. You taught me how to be kind.

Team Two, the climbers at PG, you have supported my journey the last sixteen years. Your passion has built what PG has become. The best part of our story is being written.

Dr. Joe, Conquistador to King! I raise my glass to you, *señor*. Love ya, Doc.

Jim, you changed my life. I will pay your generosity forward.

Pat, your fables pulled me up the mountain. Every aspiring leader needs your work.

Amy, you read the first version and encouraged me every step of the way. *Gracias!*

Bill, you always shoot me straight. You can't run from this compliment, *señor!* Grateful.

Dennis, at our first dinner you asked when the book was coming. You're a big reason it's here.

To my army of mentors: the advice you have given me— and most importantly, the time you have given me— was priceless. Your belief in me always gave me hope.

Davia, you rock, *señorita!* Your gift for storytelling inspires me.

Todd, the more excited you became about this book during this journey, the more nervous I became. I'm now as excited about the friendship we will develop as I am about this book.

Ray, thanks for jumping on board, and I know I'm going to feel the same about you. *Gracias!*

A Bard Press book
Publisher: Ray Bard
Deputy Publisher: Todd Sattersten
Substantive Editor: Davia Larson
Copyeditor: Sarah Currin-Moles
Proofreading: Leah Brown and Deborah Costenbader
Text Design and Production: Joy Stauber, Stauber Brand Studio
Jacket Design: Joy Stauber, Stauber Brand Studio
Illustrations: Chuck Gonzales

Many thanks to our early readers who provided
valuable comments and recommendations:
Whitney Barton, Joe Bogar, Scott Carter, Joe Currier,
Frank DeCastro, Lisa Faithorn, Clint Greenleaf,
Josh Hauser, Ed Herrera, Amy Hiett, Melissa Lombard,
Tom Mehl, Jay Papasan, Jen Pasquier, Jack Phillips,
Toby Quinton, Bill Soteroff, Jim Talbot

The Gift of Struggle: Life-Changing Lessons About Leading
Bobby Herrera

Published by Bard Press, Austin, Texas

Bard Press
info@bardpress.com — www.bardpress.com

Ordering Information
For additional copies, contact your favorite bookstore or email
info@bardpress.com. Quantity discounts are available.

ISBN-13: 9781885167873
ISBN-10: 1885167873

Publisher's Cataloging-in-Publication Data

Names: Herrera, Bobby, author. | Gonzales, Chuck, illustrator.
Title: The gift of struggle : [life-changing lessons about leading] / by Bobby
    Herrera ; [illustrations: Chuck Gonzales].
Description: First edition. | Austin, Texas : Bard Press, [2019] | Subtitle from
    copyright page. | "A Bard Press book."
Identifiers: ISBN 9781885167873 | ISBN 1885167873 | ISBN 9781885167880
    (ebook)
Subjects: LCSH: Herrera, Bobby--Career in business--Anecdotes. |
    Leadership--Anecdotes. | LCGFT: Anecdotes.
Classification: LCC HD57.7 .H47 2019 (print) | LCC HD57.7 (ebook) |
    DDC 658.4092--dc23

First Edition: First Printing, June 2019

One Final Note

Dear Reader,

It would be great to hear from you.

If you want to share one
of your gifts of struggle,
send me a note at:
hello@bobby-herrera.com

All Hail the Underdogs,

Bobby